# Free Verse Editions

Edited by Jon Thompson

# Free Verse Editions

Edited by Jon Thompson

2008

*Quarry* by Carolyn Guinzio
*Between the Twilight and the Sky* by Jennie Neighbors
*The Prison Poems* by Miguel Hernández,
    translated by Michael Smith
*remanence* by Boyer Rickel
*What Stillness Illuminated* by Yermiyahu Ahron Taub

2007

*Child in the Road* by Cindy Savett
*Verge* by Morgan Lucas Schuldt
*The Flying House* by Dawn-Michelle Baude

2006

*Physis* by Nicolas Pesque, translated by Cole Swensen
*Puppet Wardrobe* by Daniel Tiffany
*These Beautiful Limits* by Thomas Lisk
*The Wash* by Adam Clay

2005

*A Map of Faring* by Peter Riley
*Signs Following* by Ger Killeen
*Winter Journey* [Viaggio d'inverno] by Attilio Bertolucci,
    translated by Nicholas Benson

# Between the Twilight and the Sky

Jennie Neighbors

Parlor Press
West Lafayette, Indiana
www.parlorpress.com

Parlor Press LLC, West Lafayette, Indiana 47906

Printed in the United States of America
S A N: 2 5 4 - 8 8 7 9

Library of Congress Cataloging-in-Publication Data

Neighbors, Jennie.
  Between the twilight and the sky / Jennie Neighbors.
      p. cm. -- (Free verse editions)
  ISBN 978-1-60235-087-8 (pbk. : acid-free paper) -- ISBN 978-1-
60235-088-5 (adobe ebook)
  I. Title.
  PS3614.E4425B48 2008
  811'.6--dc22
                                        2008041922

Epigraph: "De moment en moment" by René Char in *Le Bâton de
    rosier*. Editions Gallimard, Paris. Used by permission of Marie-
    Claude Char.
Author photograph by Jim Neighbors. Used by permission.
Cover photograph "Signor Farini—Rope Ascension" © 1859, Filing
    #D417685, Niagara Falls Heritage Foundation Collection. Used
    by permission.
Printed on acid-free paper.

Parlor Press, LLC is an independent publisher of scholarly and trade
titles in print and multimedia formats. This book is available in
paper and Adobe eBook formats from Parlor Press on the World
Wide Web at http://www.parlorpress.com or through online and
brick-and-mortar bookstores. For submission information or to
find out about Parlor Press publications, write to Parlor Press, 816
Robinson St., West Lafayette, Indiana, 47906, or e-mail editor@
parlorpress.com.

for Jim and Esten

# Contents

## Canto II
## Between Death and Beauty  31

## Canto III
## In the Lock of Artist Time  59

# Between the Twilight and the Sky

How can we show, without betraying them, the simple things sketched between the twilight and the sky? By virtue of stubborn life, in the lock of artist Time, between death and beauty.

*—René Char*

# Canto I

## By Virtue of Stubborn Life

# Three Towns and an
# Abstract Universal

"A doctrine of connectedness is wanted.
It is how the past lives in the present.
It is causation. It is memory.
How the past perishes is how the future becomes."


But then again, too many is's ruin a good game.


"an unraveling
               of its limits: a paradoxical
individuation
               by indetermination"

# Of Its Own Accord

                    and this

crazy azalea bursts
into flame:


how the past perishes
how the future becomes

# The Problem of Freedom

present in the trees'
rings, and the leaves fall

between

the traces

sung

by Mnemosyne, washed

by Lethe

the question
we formulate on its behalf

the past perishes

# The Problem of Freedom

present in the trees'
rings, the leaves fall
-ing, each day


(affection

answers to the question

# The Problem of Freedom

                                    leaves fall

each day
differs                from itself

every moment:


(affection: polysemy without mask, this

corresponding

# Song of Secret Hymns

"If they are bastards...it is not due to a mixing or inter-mingling of languages, but rather to a subtraction and variation...."


An exchange of questions and answers between the heart and eyes. Leveled thus, this little monad went to market.

Let's not fool ourselves.

The final moment quiet as all get out. That which seeks to limit only displaces further.

horizon/orison


"knowledge is a treasury and
your heart is
its strong-box (cor tuum archa)"

## As the Present Writing Speaks

"letters are shapes indicating voices...
frequently they speak voicelessly the utterances of the absent"

"The gift of writing is precisely what writing refuses."

# Untitled

the snow falls
like seedtufts from a cottonwood

the notes of a Bach fugue gather and disperse


to keep silence

# Of Its Own Accord

late September and this
                              bursts

under the falling leaves

# The Fool

the smooth unpolished face
                                of the lute
its round back
                        pressed against
his chest


he acknowledges you with his eyes

turned away

## The Bookcase: A Prelude

from across
at some point
        not boundless

that it goes on

(I will stay with
what is near to me, where the heat
                    rises...

perhaps

I am certain

the air folds away
answers to each other
anyone

      porous as they are

"crammed with heaven" just as everything is

just as everything is
mostly emptiness

"I have nothing to say, and I am saying it...."

## The Vinculum

just spoken, the word
divides
                            the parts
                which are not one

each part folded in on                     and stretches backwards

faster than light, into the future:

encircle, fold back in, limitless:


just spoken, the word
divides, the limit

            of it, just now, raveling
into darkness



our eye already
the spoken

## Song of Secret Hymns

we follow this road: where we were became impassible

bone, top, ball, tambourine, apples, mirror, fan and fleece,
compass and square: a ligament, a bond or tie: trenches,
furrows, gaps between fences, paths into forests, cross-
roads, the place between high and low tide,

        "once upon a time,"

                  "it was and was not so"

the eidos of
        determinate space, the face
                of the outside


Legba, Oedipus, werewolves, witches...

# Thought

       outside edge
of the inside

fits

    and starts


Landscapes are preparation for what will later appear as a
set.
A certain number a story always slips into, or tends to.

# Videndo Legant

Not only is (the painting) an isolated reality, but it also
implies the relationship in a composite whole.

It must be clear and precise, recorded precisely, like what
Giacometti did:

six truths in a matchbox.


If you can read this, you're too close.

It is not you. But your voice echoes in them.


(foreigner in your own tongue)

# A Lesson From Bach

the notes
        falling over each other

to get there first
        to vanish first


into the thickening air

# Bone, Top, Ball

that they change, or that
something changes

Mnemosyne
Lethe
Hermes, the deliverer

then a rose, then a lofty speech
ever lucid over
                          homeward
another

body in an image, not another
image of a body

glorious
body

returns: for a glimpse
and a sip of water: turned

the time between: a contracted *thus*
          gemlike

                          the water
you taste is tears

of water: a contracted
*thus*

thus turned
to salt

mirror world, one
of them, but which?

shapes indicating voices bring to mind
through the windows of the eyes


(cor tuum archa)


(poling the river)

# Cor Tuum Archa

what enters in

    a rhythm             a discord

keep it soft

a line from eye
to eye

knowledge is always
knowledge
           of

# Opens the Horizon

This would be about sunset—the coming of night; the pressure, the progression of light.

# To the Night of the World

when shadow rises out of itself
posits itself
like a footprint
                 or lamppost, even

the light trembles


limited only by perception and
ability to endure it, say "friend" and enter

# The Shore

"...is the sun rising or setting?
So what! You can rest here on the shore"

Gunnar Ekelöf

Where words climb
and do not climb,

themselves—

and call to mind, and do not
call to mind,

breath and body, their sea-

sounds not quite
but almost

drowning out

the inevitable rattle

resting here, where this sea speaks
and does not

speak, its secrets—

which may, or may not, be

# Pictures of the Sea

watercurl,
                    lightsplatter,

instant (how small
must the moment be

for us to say, here it is


—among momentary days—


"Another touch with the thumb," said Giacometti,
"and whoops!—no more figure."

## Gran Chemin

and

                              moving into
the path between
you meet to become the world that is
illumined is
the very thing

that leads, in the evening, when certainty disappears

the tiny displacement, love, the entering
and the entered: Legba, road and gate

# The Act

light flecks, shook foil

and if this light opens
from the "perhaps" and

if this opens

gaps, the sky
     darkens, runs
into darkness


—but the darkness does away with all that—


the earth sinks into it
eye catches
     last light

# A Life

hurling itself into a new fact

the longing, the idea, the promise

—desire is an added thing
that unsettles, or a subtracted thing that unravels

to blend, to make itself whatever

# Canto II

# Between Death and Beauty

# The Capacity for Power

the leaf does not tremble
the leaf is a traversing

# The Capacity for Power

tremble because of
the wind, a traversing of

the uninhabitable

# The Capacity for Power

the leaf of the uninhabitable
trembles

when all is said
is the encounter called world

being stubborn with a word,
we two are made to meet and

we are the parting of two who meet
in our disparity, our resistance, because the frame

slips: Legba enters with his limp

## Precisely In its Failure, Language Succeeds

between two uninhabitable states
left without language

tremble of desire
tremble of fear

# Capacity

between the unimaginable and the incomplete

a door of the world opening on itself

a sprig with its flower
                              I break

# Capacity

affection in

               the interval's
restlessness
of skin, sky's
          capacity
for incompleteness
               power

beneath the light it rejects
                  the object

forest light like water

# Trembling

because of the wind
the leaf is

at any moment
pried open by the vibration of

a violin string or whatever else, freed for an instant from,
and shimmering, stark, in its factuality and passage

with its flower           to carry us over
chaos and cosmos, byss and abyss, flow and reflexivity, to
one another


welter of world


for beauty is nothing but the beginning,
the emptiness from your arms

## Between Death and Beauty

the indeterminate
singing at the edges       the crystal rim
                     and the winewet fingertip

everything is the traversed and the traversing

of the tremble: between
     the notes (once again)
            "affection shall solve the problems of
    freedom yet"

# Morning Song

Gives rise, this rising and this falling, a rising and darker
world.
A morning song so fledged it can include the long shad-
ows of itself.

You stand where you are, the only unendurable instant,
losing the thread.


—a song for us, so fledged

# Dawn

one could conceive of such a pleasure

# The Country of the Night

For several nights, a single treefrog singing, its birdclear note disappearing, filling the darkness with the anticipation of it.

Or was it the nightingale, hidden in the gray shadows?

Soon the night air will be filled with the sound of crickets, too.

# Hermes

like a river announcing its depth and extremity
as if transforming itself into night,
the very thing that leads

with its flower
I

# Syntax; or, What the Poem Thinks of Death

to get to the end before the beginning disappears

perhaps

who would take leave of all faith and every wish
thus so fledged
that it will and chase away
on insubstantial ropes

such a pleasure and power
who will sing
the art of a song for us, so sunny,
so light and its further darkness will

# Between Death and Beauty

winewet

everything is

affection

# What the Poem Thinks of Death

                 plume and froth
catching
                 light, rippling
out among
                 the pink blossoms


such a small thing
this longing

because there is something else
or because there is not

the wrens' nest silent

wingflutter glance
across closed eyes

## What the Poem Thinks of Death

above the blossoms, browned and windblown,

the tightrope walker


unable to pause


thus
all the while

passing through

# What the Poem Can Carry

silences, not silence:

sonorous rests          of

worlds, logics, words

# What the Poem Cannot Carry

the one, the nothing
the exaltation of the masochist
      headed for battle


(but always open to escape, traveler,

sufficient to overcome)


—but the thing just hangs there, not yet entirely given in

to falling—

# After William Carlos Williams

There are no things, but in betweens.

# Homage to Creeley and Ponge

some thing as
simple
as
I speak

# While Dancing, the Dervish Sings

where is it
    the crystal lens
    the unmixed heart
and just why
    is not the snail
majestic, and if
    the shimmer-
ing interface is punctured

what's left?

# Homage to Creeley and Ponge

some thing
as

simple as
the idea such

as I
or speaks

# Death is Entirely

natural. What is unnatural
is speech
while dead—this makes one
poetic, like that bird
wings spread
                    as if
in flight

## Death is Entirely

               is entirely
      what is
   is speech
                  makes one

                as if
  in


position in relation to the ground we stand on, where we choose or happen to stand

opened up externally and internally (to interpretation, to context)


burst, by their very precision and conciseness

## Fairy Tale

a bird and a stone are tossed into the air—
the stone returns,

                           but the bird is lost...

58

# Canto III

# In the Lock of Artist Time

60

# As Found in A Short History of the Shadow

Van Gogh said "[Death] follows [artists] around like their shadows"


painting began as tracing a shadow:
something only in the instant

of difference

    there are only a few places left, bridges through,
    bridges without start or finish



plus a little light,
        plus a little dark—

## A Little Endarkment

there are only a few places left for the unbeliever

because we appeal to reason as if it were a light; because
without darkness, light dazzles; because our bodies con-
tain darknesses; because our minds contain darknesses;
because without light, darkness conceals; because purity
is loss of the multiple; because to love one thing is to not
love enough

"This mirror contains the sky, the clouds, the trees, all the
verdure and the quivering of the leaves. Everything reflects
itself in it, resumes itself in it, dissolves itself in it."

image of furrow: "the being of man": no longer, but not yet

# A Little Endarkment

                                        wholly in darkness

but that water contains the sky . . .

reflects, resumes, dissolves
itself in it

## Casting a Shadow

image of furrow,
its trick to me
                        but not yet


and words: contraband
in secret, hiding, wait

# Beauty as the Color of
# Truth, so to Speak

the haze brightens in the setting sun

in a silver bowl
thousands of mountains

why is it that

silver bowl at midnight
silver bowl at noon


following, suddenly, the swallowing of the future into the
past

# The Direction the Poem Must Travel

                    rising and falling with the horizon
chances are the found object
that you:
                    altering, destroying, etc.

the border, its shimmering edge


standing on, looking

# Night Garden

Tonight, the moon is held like snow
in a silver bowl.

We gather our words.

## Night Garden

We gather our words.

                    The sun shines brightly
framed by two twilights.

# Night Garden

in a silver bowl

elsewhere

# Labyrinth

what is the mode
what mode
    of existence
in order to be
        able
insofar as it
        blossoms

# The Attribute: Pale White

isolated from the camellia's blossom
early or late winter
translucent under ice

a half-moment
to gather it or be
gathered up


"the instant," a sufi says, "cuts the root of the future and
the past."

## A Little Endarkment

there are only a few places left


everything
                in it

# In Artist Time

the mode of
the person
       who utters any

what mode of is needed
in order to be

able to utter it?       blossom, early, under,

and—the root
of

# The Labyrinth

is a subtraction

the thread we take in, the thread we take out
unraveling, raveling
to the point, the place in time, but time
is divided time, running
both directions at once, empty time

in between

# Materials Needed

this present
in your own tongue

who speaks?

## Self-Portrait

Materials needed: pencil, paper, self, eraser, mirror
Objectives:
Directions: the same thread back, the color of sunset.

# Ariadne's Thread

extends along
the horizon: rises and falls and you

rising and falling
are it, half under

what can't be
                  assimilated, rises into, as

the instant

# Address to a Strait Line

"They say there is no Strait Line in Nature this is a Lie like all that
they say, For there is Every Line in Nature. . . ." William Blake


you must be a point
but with extension
infinitely small
folded in—

that grain of sand
strait line
that awake!

the sound of the ocean in your ears

# The Material

If the sky is restlessness, then
If the sky is restlessness and we
Our horizon and the trembling, where they meet

affection inheres

# The Aeon

in relation to: the child
who plays: is now
the time of: the game

# Twilight As

labyrinth: "palace of the two-edged axe"

the not yet and the already gone

ceaselessly, and its productions

# The Game

calls forth
cantankerous, brave,
through the fissure

the turtle, meanwhile

# The Turtle as an Aphorism

Alone in its tank. Tiny nostrils above the waterline, skin filaments still cling to its legs and wave in the water. Now it climbs atop the perch. Its throat expands and contracts.

As timbre is outside the circle of time and interval, the turtle is outside the circle of that which can be charted.

# Untitled Conditional

if I, you, now, were to
and if, then

the sky's restlessness
the earth's windblown blossoms
the traveler in between

the anomalous you must meet to become

# According to the Movement
# of a Turtle's Foot

the sun squanders
itself, sheds
itself and ends
                    up here, reflected
up through the aquarium water
where it shimmers

# Night Walk Through the Trees

as language: loses the thread
looking for another
voice—as a music that winds

# Acknowledgments

I gratefully acknowledge the editors of Ugly Duckling Presse, *Dusie, Free Verse: A Journal of Contemporary Poetry and Poetics*, and *Still Home: The Essential Poetry of Spartanburg* (Hub City Press, 2008), for including some of these poems in their pages.

I would also like to thank L. Elizabeth Bryant, Dave Rodrick, Rosa Shand, Christine Dinkins, Nathan Halverson, Mike Smith, Mark Ferguson, Jon Thompson, and David Blakesley for their generosity of time and spirit.

## *Credits*

Adonis. *The Pages of Day and Night*. The Marlboro Press, 1994.

Agamben, Giorgio. *The Coming Community*. University of Minnesota Press, 1993.

Balibar, Etienne. *Spinoza and Politics*. Verso, 1998.

Batailles, Georges. *Visions of Excess: Selected Writings, 1927-1939*. University of Minnesota, 1985.

Blake, William. *The Complete Poetry and Prose of William Blake*. Doubleday, 1988.

Blanchot, Maurice. *The Writing of the Disaster*. University of Nebraska Press, 1995.

Blaser, Robin. *The Holy Forest*. Coach House Press, 1993.

Buber, Martin. *I and Thou*. Charles Scribner's Sons, 1958.

Caillois, Roger. *Man, Play and Games*. University of Illinois Press, 2001.

Celan, Paul. *Threadsuns*. Sun & Moon Press, 2000.

Char, René. *Selected Poems*. New Directions, 1992.

Clanchy, M.T. *From Memory to Written Record: English 1066-1307*. Blackwell Publishers, 1993.

Deleuze, Gilles. *Essays Critical and Clinical*. University of Minnesota Press, 1997.

—. *The Fold: Leibniz and the Baroque*. University of Minnesota Press, 1993.

—. *Nietzsche and Philosophy*. Columbia University Press, 1983.

—. *Pure Immanence: Essays on A Life*. Zone Books, 2001.

Deleuze, Gilles, and Felix Guattari. *Kafka: Toward a Minor Literature*. University of Minnesota Press, 1986.

—. *A Thousand Plateaus: Capitalism and Schizophrenia*. University of Minnesota Press, 1987.

Deleuze, Gilles, and Claire Parnet. *Dialogues*. Columbia University Press, 1987.

Duncan, Robert. *A Little Endarkenment And In My Poetry You Find Me*. Poetry/Rare Books Collection, Rodent Press, Erudite Fang, 1997.

Ekelöf, Gunnar. *Songs of Something Else: Selected Poems of Gunnar Ekelöf*. Princeton University Press, 1982.

Foucault, Michel. *Language, Counter-Memory, Practice*. Cornell University Press, 1977.

Mitchell, W. J. T., ed. *Landscape and Power*. University of Chicago Press, 1994.

Nietzsche, Friedrich. *The Gay Science*. Random House, 1974.

Richter, Gerhard. *The Daily Practice of Painting*. Thames and Hudson, Ltd., 1995.

Rilke, Rainer Maria. *The Selected Poetry of Rainer Maria Rilke*. Vintage Books, 1989.

Stoichita, Victor I. *A Short History of the Shadow*. Reaktion Books Ltd., 1997.

Trubshaw, Bob. "The Metaphors and Rituals of Place and Time: An Introduction to Liminality." At the Edge Archive. 10 Mar. 2008 <http://www.indigogroup.co.uk/edge/liminal.htm>.

Turner, Victor. *The Anthropology of Performance*. PAJ Publications, 1987.

—. *From Ritual to Theatre: The Human Seriousness of Play*. PAJ Publications, 1982.

Whitehead, Alfred North. *Adventures of Ideas*. Free Press, 1967.

—. *Process and Reality*. Free Press, 1979.

Whitman, Walt. *Leaves of Grass*. Bantam Books, 1983.

# About the Author

Jennie Neighbors lives in Spartanburg, SC, with her husband, Jim, and son, Esten. She is a Wisconsin Arts Board Fellow, a graduate of Naropa University's MFA Program and a recipient of their Ted Berrigan Memorial Fellowship. Her poems have appeared in journals of innovative writing such as *Free Verse, Dusie, Osiris, Dirigible,* and *gestalten.* She teaches at Wofford College.

Photograph of the author by Jim Neighbors. Used by permission.

www.ingramcontent.com/pod-product-compliance
Lightning Source LLC
Chambersburg PA
CBHW032022090426
42741CB00006B/709